Overcomers!

A Study of 7 Victorious Women of the Bible

Sandra R. Jolla

TABLE OF CONTENTS

FOREWORD

"This book for me reflects much of the wisdom, inspiration and teachings of women in my life-my grandmother, my mother, my aunts, church and community women and others who have gone before me."

In the mid 1990's while speaking at a banquet in Greenville, Texas, it was my pleasure to have met a charming, friendly local pastor and his wife, Reverend Michael and Mrs. Sandra Jolla!

As the years passed, our paths seldom crossed, but there remained a bond that kept us connected. The year 2003 was the beginning of a continuous partnership as Sandra Jolla came on board as a worker with the Missionary Baptist General Convention of Texas Women and Girls' Conference! For over a decade, Sandra has coordinated and given her expertise in service to over 300 girls known as the Christian Debutantes. The impact, the passion, the exemplary service, the servant leadership combined with perfection, caring and compassion were evident. As with this project, she easily exemplifies the motto, 'giving her best in service'.

Women, in times like these, have many issues and are seeking answers. **"Overcomers"-A Study of 7 Victorious Women in the Bible"** provides the needed answers and responses. The saying, "association brings about assimilation" is so true. When we connect with others to find solutions to our problems, it often leads to powerful results.

Great comfort and resolve come in Biblical experiences, which is why we turn to our faith. We often find others in our faith walk who have set the pace, set the path. Many of us can identify with what these Trailblazers have endured and are encouraged to fulfil the old cliché.... 'if they can...I can!'.

This book is the answer to modern day Biblical Studies resulting in motivation and inspiration to live "victorious" lives. It provides a framework for women who encounter different roles in their life journeys and epitomizes women of strength and honor. Sandra Jolla's writing of 7 women, including Rizpah, a woman of bravery and a risk taker; Ester, a woman of strength, intelligence, and bravery; and Hannah, a woman of elevated self-esteem motivated by faith and prayer, depicts the various seasons in the lives of women today.

Sandra Jolla is a superb Christian woman, mother, wife, writer, talk show host, and author. Her sensitivity to the journey of women is reflective in her captivating studies of their day to day living. She is considered by many as the Proverbs 31 Woman, especially in the religious community, and as that phenomenal woman that Maya Angelou solidifies. Her revelations of these 7 Women of the Bible, offer valuable insight into her own personal struggles and triumphs in life.

ENJOY THE LIFE LESSONS!

Frances C. Worthey, PhD Waco, Texas

INTRODUCTION

"What you get by achieving your goals is not as important as what you become by achieving your goals" —*Zig Ziglar*

Life presents many opportunities for us to be inspired by the lives and works of others. It is so encouraging to find individuals who inspire and motivate even amid turbulent times. Like the women presented in this book, I am an OVERCOMER! I choose VICTORY! What a bold declaration of positive affirmation. Yet so many are often overtaken by crisis, by life, by news of failing and threatening health issues, by the enemy. Victory must be intentional. It must be an emotional drive that propels you into a mental state of winning. Webster defines victory as the overcoming of an enemy or the achievement of mastery or success in a struggle or to endeavour against odds or difficulties.

I am blessed to be victorious in so many areas of life, however I am even more humbled to know that it was not me alone, who provided such a sweet savour of victory in so many areas of my life. I praise God that I have been blessed to have so many women who inspired me each step along the way of my journey. I praise God further for the richness of my relationship with Him, which provided biblical examples of women with issues, with everyday situations that they too, had to deal with.

The Bible is so rich with living examples of people who had to deal with life issues. I have chosen seven women who frame much of my life's story.

A story rich with experiences, motivation, faith, and love. I am so grateful that I started a "real" walk with Christ early in my professional career. I am eternally grateful to my friend Randi Miles, Oscar and Linda Roan who helped to quench my deep desire to know and study more about God through the rich home Bible Study formed in my mid-twenties; and then to the Munger Avenue Baptist Church and Rev. Dr. Barry Jackson who challenged my learning and taught me how to dig deeper to understand the richness of God's Word. And even more now, with my Pastor and husband, Rev. Dr. Michael A. Jolla who challenges us weekly to dig deeper for the "truths" of God's Word. I will never forget women like Mrs. Deloris Brooks and Mrs. Kathryn Moore who showed me Biblical principle and beyond that, how important it is to also be living examples, as they were of Christian women to emulate. Women of integrity, who demonstrated love, caring, and sharing for God's people.

Whether the richness of Hannah's prayer; the prompt decision-making of Abigail; the depth of friendship through Ruth with her relationship with Naomi; the success of being a business woman with principles and ethics, as Lydia; the richness of having the honour of being a mother who would reach the level of devotion and sacrificial love for her children as Rizpah or the faith of the Syrophoenician woman to persevere even though the blessing seemed impossible. I am so thankful to God for providing these Biblical examples, but also for placing women in my life; women who exude the character and traits of these women.

Starting with my beloved mother, Mrs. Gloria Grant Reese Philpot who gave the unwavering and sacrificial love of Rizpah. She worked 2 jobs, went to college and stayed up sewing clothes for me and my sister many times into the early morning hours to show us a better life. What a sacrifice?

She not only demonstrated perseverance, but showed me that with a positive attitude, and right motives you can achieve anything in life. Such principles I live by even to this day! I praise God for such women as Betty Reese, Brenda Jones, Sheila Reese, Vantrice Jackson, Valerie York, Jeanette Jones, and Leatra Holmes whose deep and abiding love for their children are a magnificent model of motherhood.

Each chapter of the book starts with women who have inspired me somewhere along my life's journey. The intent is to not only study the Biblical truths of the women of the Bible, but to highlight women who have been instrumental in my life in demonstrating the character of the women we will study. This is an effort to show women of God, that they too can be role models, living examples of the women God blessed in these stories to be a beacon of hope for others. I challenge each of you to ask yourself, am I a woman who is an example for women to emulate?

While the story of each of these women is intriguing, the intent is to pull out the character and truths that each of the women possess that will help us build our Christian character, our faith and our Christian walk.

The women are presented in alphabetical order, and not necessarily the degree of impact they had on me or their stories. It is my sincere prayer, that some woman when she studies this book is so enlightened, as I was during the various periods of my life, when these women came to life for me in dealing with the issues I had along life's way. If not, these seven women, find one which best relates to you and what you are dealing with. The Bible is rich with women. To name a few others, Mary, the mother of Jesus; Phoebe, the servant. Miriam, Bathsheba, Elizabeth and so many others!

I asked and am grateful that seven women who have been instrumental to me in demonstrating the character of these women have agreed to write an introduction to each of the chapters, based on at least one of the traits demonstrated by the women they are introducing.

While I would love to call the names of so many other women who have been instrumental in my life, like many women in my church, time and pages will not allow. I am so grateful for Dr. Frances C. Worthey, Director of Women's Ministry for the Missionary Baptist General Convention of Texas (MBGCT) for her leadership, grace and always giving spirit which has impacted me in so many ways. She entrusted me to be the Debutante Coordinator for the MBGCT for the past 13 years.

Impacting the lives of over 300 young ladies speaks volume to not only the opportunity but the chance to make a positive impact on these young and tender girl's lives. For this I am so eternally grateful!

Mrs. Hazel Jeane Thomas, Curriculum Developer and Teacher for the Missionary Baptist General Convention of Texas (MBGCT) Women's Ministry, who provided my first opportunity to teach and develop curriculum which stretched me and gave me the confidence and faith to continue on a path of passionately teaching God's Word and inspiring women.

Hattie Tennison whose unwavering faith and 'can do' attitude propelled us as she was the administrative assistant to my husband for his first pastoral calling. Her stamina, support, friendship and demonstrated love will forever be etched in the chronicles of my life!

To my friends of over 40 years, Evelyn Holmes and Randi Miles who I met when I was a single woman living in Dallas, Texas all by myself. You don't know how much you value friendship and family until you are presented with the opportunity to leave all you know and love and chart a path of friendship and a bond that parallels the family and friendship you can no longer readily embrace because of distance. These ladies demonstrated then and continue to be the bonds that tie friendship together for me and are the godmothers for my beautiful daughters, Brasha and Brianna.

I love these women to the moon and back, for there is nothing that I could ask that they would not come to my rescue, and I do not take this friendship lightly. For this reason, I want to also lift up my dear friends Vantrice Jackson, Gale Johnson and certainly my "Lab High" girlfriends- Barbara Franklin, Carole Burton, Tondalaire Ashford, Alma Arrington, Kathy Sawyer, Marcia Rivers, Arwilla Chattom, Samuetta Nesbitt, Bobbetta Jones and Audrey Anderson-truly women who are friends for life!

Service also plays an important role in who I am and how I choose to execute the calling God has on my life. As such, I am an active member of the Alpha Kappa Alpha Sorority, Incorporated®, currently Alpha Tau Omega Chapter, San Antonio, Texas. Our motto is service to all mankind and we pride ourselves on fulfilling the philanthropic needs of all people. While I have been blessed to serve with many dynamic and motivating women in this organization like Beverly Long, Evelyn Hamilton, Dr. Tania Jackson; the one who has made the most impact with me in service is H. Donna Millhouse, former President of Alpha Tau Omega Chapter. Her creative sense of community and service was amazing, and I appreciate the opportunity to execute so many successful programs under her tutelage.

And then, out of my 38+ years in the business world, and of all of the outstanding women I had the pleasure to work with, I am so grateful to Melinda Chausse, Sr. VP at a Financial Institution who I had the pleasure to work with for 8 years. I was motivated beyond measure as a business professional to work with a woman of such high moral and ethical standards. Like Lydia, she is a woman who is respected by many and whose ability to be kind and considerate while dealing with tough business issues was so encouraging and motivating to me. Because she set the bar high, I was able to aim high and I appreciate that.

I pray that this book will be a blessing and resource to Women's Ministry and Study Groups. Each chapter reviews the lesson, central points of the lesson and provides a lesson teaching plan and discussion guide with intriguing questions or "food for thought" for Bible Study Leaders. Each story provides reaffirming assurance that when the Lord is with you, there is no issue we cannot overcome. I pray that you will be as motivated to study these OVERCOMERS as I have been studying them.

Although not a woman, I must give homage to my best friend, motivator, and partner! To God be the Glory for Rev. Dr. Michael A. Jolla, my Pastor, husband, and unbelievable supporter. I am so blessed to have been chosen as his soulmate and I am deeply appreciative of the two beautiful daughters Brasha and Brianna that God has allowed me to mother and the life I have experienced as the first Lady of the "House of Jolla" and the "Exciting" West End Baptist Church.

Sisterly Yours,
Sandra

WISDOM IS FROM GOD

The fear of the Lord is the beginning of knowledge, but fools despise wisdom and instruction.—Proverb 1:7(NIV)

The troubling times in which we face, demand us as Christians to not only be acquainted with God's plan for salvation: but instructed, knowledgeable, and full of wisdom so that our walk matches our talk. It is especially important for us to remember *God is our refuge in these troubling times.* We must be cognizant and powerfully aware that wisdom is more than being knowledgeable. Utilization of God's gift of wisdom is our only hope to offset the demands of this present age.

Knowledge is determined by what we know about a certain fact or state of being. **Wisdom** is our ability to utilize that knowledge in an effective way, realizing that man knows how to acquire knowledge, **but the fear of the Lord is the beginning of wisdom.** One author stated, "Learning and remembering Bible verses about wisdom unlocks the keys to gaining insight for your Christian walk; therefore, as Christians, we can gain knowledge through the study of God's word...." wisdom from above is first pure, then peaceable, gentle, open to reason, full of mercy and good fruits, impartial and sincere" (James 3:17). Hence, let us ask God for wisdom to navigate whatever the circumstances that may occur.

Hazel Jeane Thomas, Curriculum Development
Missionary Baptist Convention of Texas,
Women's Ministry

ABIGAIL

Primary Scriptures: 1 Samuel 25:1-42
Reference Scriptures: Proverbs 14; Psalm 37

Read the Scripture:

Introduction:

God desires women whose inward actions drive their outward beauty. Which one of these would you say you use the most? Your smile, your personality, your intellect, or your overall looks.

Setting: Samuel dies, and David leaves and goes into the wilderness in the same area that Nabal lives.

[Maon is in the Judean hill country and Carmel is located on the edge of the Judean wilderness, approximately one-mile North of Maon] It was a time of sheep shearing. Many times, sheep shearing was a festive and happy occasion. This is the setting for our lesson. David and his men needed supplies as they were fleeing the threatening hand of former King Saul, and find themselves in Carmel at a time when Nabal was shearing his thousands of sheep.

Three main characters:

- Abigail: wise, intelligent and beautiful.
- Nabal: Abigail husband—surly and mean.
- David: newly appointed king of Israel

THE STORY

The story of Abigail is proof point of what God can do when women who fear the LORD are willing to use their God given gifts for good. When women are driven to cooperate with the Spirit of the LORD, with a willing and respectful attitude, God shows His hand of compassion and love. Because of her respectful behaviour, good judgement and resounding beauty, God sustained Abigail and gave her solace during very adverse and trying circumstances.

The story of Abigail is found in the book of 1 Samuel.

Even though most religious scholars do not agree on the author of 1 Samuel and the dating of the book, they do agree on its theme and its purpose. As for the name of the book, it is titled after the prophetic leader and judge Samuel, whom God used to establish an affiliation with Israel at a time when they were struggling with whether they wanted the LORD to be their guide and king, or if they wanted to follow a human king. It looks at the calling of the prophet, judge, and priesthood of Samuel, and the calling and the reign of Israel's first king, Saul and their second king, David.

The story of Abigail begins in chapter 25. In 1 Samuel 25:1, Samuel the prophet dies, and the nation of Israel laments the death *of this great prophet and judge. This story takes place at a pivotal point in the life of God's people and the transitioning of leadership.*

David has just been reluctantly acknowledged by Saul as Israel's newest king. Samuel the prophet dies and is buried in Ramah, and David leaves fleeing Saul to minimize discourse and goes down to the wilderness of Paran. While there in the wilderness, in the land of Maon and Carmel, David and his men run low on supplies and reached out for help to a rich man in the area by the name of Nabal. In I Samuel 25:2, the Bible states *that Nabel had 3000 sheep, one thousand goats, and that he sheared his sheep in the land. He was "well off".*

There are three primary characters in this story. Abigail, who is described as **"intelligent and beautiful;"** Her husband Nabal, who is mentioned in I Samuel 25:3, as one who is **"surly and mean"** in his dealings and who refused to provide for David and his men when they were passing through and were low on supplies; and King David who in I Samuel 25:33, is identified as one who allows the **grace of God** to intervene at a time when he was about to destroy Nabal, his entire family along with his estate for not helping the king and his men. There is no doubt that Abigail's inward character superseded her outward beauty. This story also shows how she used sound judgement and wisdom to not only aid the Lord's king, but also to help save her people. Proverbs 31:30-31 states, *"charm is deceitful, and beauty is fleeting, but a woman who fears the Lord is to be praised" NIV.* It is evident that Abigail uses both her brain and her beauty to be a blessing to King David and save her household.

God is looking for women who can use their "brain power" to maintain high moral standards and ethical character as well as their physical attributes. **Abigail demonstrates that inward character strengthens outward beauty.**

Her ability to see beyond her scoundrel husband, proves that she had more working for her than her beauty. In 1 Samuel 25:14-17, when she was told by one of Nabal's young servant men how her husband Nabal, insulted and treated David and His men, by ignoring his request for aid, she quickly interceded on behalf of her stubborn husband.

The Bible says, in I Samuel 25:18. *Then Abigail made haste {did not waste any time} to meet David.* Even though her husband had refused to show gratitude for the protection that David's men had shown for his herd, Abigail met him to show great appreciation and respect to her king.

"This Scripture teaches us, that even though she was a beautiful woman, it was her **intelligence** in knowing when to act; her ability to **intercede** on behalf of her stubborn husband, and her **intuition to invite** King David's men to celebrate, when her husband had refused to demonstrate kindness and wisdom saved her and her household. This story provides a worthy example of how Christian women should use their God-given wisdom and compassion in making good decisions.

Little is known about Abigail's parentage or genealogy but it is obvious that she had been taught about her Jewish history. In knowing how to respect the king, knowing that the LORD— Jehovah was her creator, caretaker, covenant making God.

It is evident, that she certainly understood protocol, and had respect for Jewish authority, and last, one could see in her speech, that she was a woman with Godly character.

See 1 Samuel 25:30-31, Even though nothing is said about how she and her brutal husband Nabal were united, it is apparent that they had contrasting character and belief systems.

Look at her behavior; led by the Spirit, servant of the LORD, attitude of gratitude and respect for her king. Her husband on the other hand: stubborn, a scoundrel, greedy, and foolish.

They remind me of the fairy tale, "Beauty and the Beast." Not only does this story invite us to look at Abigail's beauty and her brain, but it also gives us an opportunity to **explore her boldness and her blessings. What happens when we are not led by God, but by our own selfish, scoundrel and stubborn desire?** We find that even knowing of her husband's brutal acts of unkindness and his desire to be selfish, Abigail was willing to go against his ungodly character and brutal behavior of her husband for the betterment of her household.

Abigail had to take action and risk abuse from her husband, to ensure that King David would not destroy her entire household. The Scripture describes Nabal in I Samuel 25:3 as *"surly and mean in his dealings.* Proverbs 1:5 states "let the wise listen and add their learning." It is apparent that Nabal was not willing to listen, not to King David, his servant, nor his wife.

Abigail had a difficult decision. She had to decide whether she was going to side with her husband, Nabal, one whom the Bible says was a fool, or to decide to show respect to the newly appointed king of the land—King David. I Kings 25: 25-28, It is also evident, by Nabal's actions, that he was not willing to acknowledge David as king of the land, and that he was not appreciative of the guarded protection that had been given by David's men in protecting his herd—his 3000 sheep and his 1000 goats. Instead, he chose to demonstrate his stubborn and ill-tempered behavior by refusing to allow David's men refuge even though they had protected his sheep without incidence, I Samuel 25:7-13.

Because of her husband's actions and ways, Abigail, a woman of dignity, class, humility, and wisdom stood boldly in the gap to intercede on his behalf as David and his men took aim to destroy him and his household. In effect, Abigail put her **sole trust in God** and threw herself in harm's way to save her ruthless husband and her household. What a woman of character!

When she meets King David, she demonstrates a spirit of servanthood [she presented herself as a maidservant] and expresses an **attitude of gratitude**, 1 Samuel 25: 20-24. Many times, God just needs willing vessels, who will humble themselves and express gratitude for acknowledgement of his blessings and to show acts of kindness.

With such a bold act of courage, Abigail took a chance that doing good would yield good results.

She quickly acted and interceded as if the spirit within her thrust her forward. Immediately, she sought to meet David's militia, carrying two hundred loaves of bread, two skins of wine, five dressed sheep, five seahs of roasted grain, a hundred cakes of raisins, and two hundred cakes of pressed   figs to overly compensate for her husband's ill-behaviour.

Of course, she knew she could not share this plan with her ruthless husband. **Many times, we fail to seek God's divine goodness instead, we sulk in our despair.**

The Bible says in I Samuel 25:32, because of her kindness, King David showed mercy. And David said to Abigail *"Praise be to the Lord, the God of Israel, who has sent you today to meet me"*. Because of Abigail's intercessory actions on behalf of her husband, she and her household are spared from destruction. The Apostle Paul writes in 2 Corinthian 12:9, *My grace is sufficient for thee: for My strength is made perfect in weakness. Most gladly therefore, will I rather glory in my infirmities, that the power of Christ may rest upon me.* Yes, God's grace is sufficient and will cover us amid our trying and troubling times. If we just find the courage to surrender our causes to Him.

What happens when a woman intercedes on behalf of her household?

I am sure Abigail was overjoyed with her success with the king and desired to share this good news with her husband, however upon her return home, she finds him drunk and out of sound mind. Again, she demonstrates good judgement and godly character waiting until the next day when he is sober to share the news of her success. Ecclesiastes reminds us in 3:1 *"To everything there is a season, and a time to every purpose under the heaven"*: 7b-8, ***"a time to keep silent, and a time to speak;*** 8: *A time to love, and a time to hate; a time of war, and a time of peace."* Yes, to everything, there is a right season, and a right time, within that season.

Paralyzed by the news, Nabal suffers a heart attack and dies ten days later. When David heard the news, he rejoiced and sent for Abigail to become his wife. In the twinkling of an eye, she went from a viciously brutal to a blessed relationship.

The adage says, 'it is no secret what God can do, what He's done for others, he'll do for you' comes to mind. Was it really the news, or was it that the day finally came when his scoundrel and stubborn ways finally caught up with him? Was it because the Lord blessed the rightful actions of his wife, and cursed him? Or was it because of David's decision of having a forgiving spirit because of Nabal's wife?

What would you say is the moral of this story?

When was the last time that you had to intercede for your household?

POINTS OF EMPHASIS:

Introduction:

- Abigail was a Godly woman who did not possess the same character as her surly husband.

- As women who are willing to follow the Lord, we must be careful of the men we encounter along life's journey and their impact on our lives.

- How can her example of godly character be a blueprint for us in times of turbulence and trouble?

- Should a wife share everything with her husband? Can you think of any situation, in which it would be best to be silent?

- We must be careful of "knowing everything" and "listening to none"! How often are we like Nabal?

- Greed will cause us to misalign and misappropriate the grace of God.

- When was the last time that you knowingly had to intercede for someone you love? Was it a favourable, or an unfavourable outcome?

THINK ABOUT IT!

- We must be mindful of the gifts that God has given us. What gift would you say that God has given you?
- Abigail used her intellect along with her beauty.
- What is the danger if I focus on using my looks alone to execute a Godly plan?
- What caused Abigail to intercede?
- How did she use her **Intelligence?**
- What could have happened if she did not Intercede?

Invitation

- Why do you think Abigail was so eager to worship David with her giving when her husband was not willing to share his wealth at all?
- How do you act when faced with a tough decision?
- What are some things that causes us not to act in tough situations?
- Why did Abigail have a difficult decision to make? Do we always make good choices?
- Proverbs 3:6, says "In all thy ways acknowledge Him, and He will direct your path."
- What harm could David do to Abigail?
- Did Abigail take a chance in asking David to forgive her husband?
- The Lord identifies who has authority. one who has ownership. Abigail acknowledges that David was now king of the land. But the LORD was king over David.

- How eager are we to forgive? Do we seek forgiveness; are we always willing to forgive?

- What would you say it takes to have a forgiving heart, a forgiving spirit?
- Abigail a woman of Godly character and a woman who knew how to respect both the LORD and those in authority. How can we apply this is our workplace, our church?

The Teaching Plan

Opening Student Involvement:
Would you prefer beauty or brains? Why?

_____

_____

Can you have both?

_____

_____

Why do we, as a society, focus so much on beauty?_____

TRUTHS OF LESSON:

Abigail, had BOTH brains and beauty. She did not let vain beauty get in the way of her witness. She is a woman who knew who and to whom to act, when to act, and how to act. She had trouble on many fronts:

- Dealing with an abusive husband.
- Sometimes we must intercede on behalf of our household.
- It is important to know when to speak to an unruly husband
- She acted with good judgment and Christian character. Because of her actions, King David spared her life and the life of her ungrateful husband.

Following are the truths to be highlighted in this lesson:
Her **Beauty** and **her Brains** – v. 3 Points of Discussion:

- Real beauty comes from within.
- Strong character is derived from having a meek and quiet spirit.

- God grants us wisdom – Proverbs 1:5.
- Productive actions yield meaningful results.
- Intelligence strengthens your overall beauty.
- Inward character strengthens outward beauty,

Her **Brutal** husband – v. 3, 10, 36
- A surly (rude) and negative disposition leads to destruction– Proverbs 14:3
- A Selfish attitude brings risks to you and your loved ones
- A Sinful nature leads your mind to sinful desires

Her **Boldness** – **v. 14-25**
- Taking a chance at doing good, many times will yield good results
- There is a benefit to addressing issues and not allowing them to linger
- Her battle v.17
- Her belief – good will come to one who is good Psalm 112:5

Her **Behavior** – v.18
- The importance of knowing protocol and respecting authority
- She demonstrated discreet tact. She knew when to speak v. 36B

Her **Blessing** – v. 39-42; Psalm 37
- David's vindication Psalm 37
- Tragedy turned to triumph
- Married David

The **Recipe** from Abigail's Life Book:
1. TRUST IN THE LORD
2. DO GOOD
3. STAND FOR RIGHT, WHEN FACED WITH

WRONG

The Lesson in Action:

CONTRAST ABIGAIL and NABAL

Abigail	Nabal
Wise /intelligent – Proverbs 14:16	Mean & Surly Proverbs 14:17
Led by the spirit	Unappreciative
Attitude of Gratitude	Contempt toward God's servant
Servant	Selfish & Self-Centered
Smart	Ungrateful
God sent - Good	Wicked

Your self-evaluation:

Circle the characteristics which most describe your character?

Will you commit today to change your Nabal like qualities and magnify your Abigail like qualities?

PRAYER:

Notes Page:

ESTHER- A WOMAN OF COMMUNITY AND HERITAGE

In life we encounter leadership roles when we least expect it. Too often, we run for office or agree to lead an effort and/or organization because our friends and/or cohorts influence us to do so. Academia has created and identified various leadership styles: Autocratic, democratic, and laissezfaire just to name a few. No matter which leadership style you adopt, I firmly believe the quality of one's leadership success totally rests in the arms of God through his Divine Providence.

A true leader is one who has a vision or is given a vision that *inspires, motivates, and leads people by personal example ...* even when it seems impossible. As a leader I confronted the challenges of leadership with **Romans 10:11**: "Whoever believes in Him will not be disappointed" (NASB). God's Divine Providence is the key to successful and meaningful leadership even in the face of impossibilities.

The word providence comes from the Latin word *providentia* meaning foresight, prudence, or the ability to look ahead. Therefore, divine Providence is God's supreme power to foresee *where and when* one's leadership will be needed unbeknownst to the person being called to the leadership mission.

Consequently, I personally hold to the concept that leaders are more successful when it is *"their time more than when they think it is their turn".* Divine Providence is rooted in God's timing and not when we think it is our turn.

During the two years I served as President of the Alpha Tau Omega Chapter of Alpha Kappa Alpha Sorority, Incorporated ®, I believe it was God's timing that placed me in that leadership position for a time such as that. Our chapter had served our community for 87 years but needed a renewal and revival of its communal position. I did not know what was in store for me, but God covered me with his Divine Providence and gave me the vision for the chapter's signature motto: *"**In the Community, By the Community and For the Community"**.* From a community standpoint this motto reminded us that we:

- Were deeply rooted the community
  (In the Community).
- Had a proven history of accomplishment
  (By the Community).
- Had a sense of duty to continue support
  (For the Community).

As I executed my duties, I began to see similarities in our motto with the story of Esther

- She was deeply rooted with her people.
- She had a proven history of accomplishment, and
- She had a sense of duty to continue her support of her people.

Leadership is challenging but the right person in the right place can change the world. Faith does not make your leadership journey easy… It makes it possible.

H. Donna Millhouse, President (2018-2019)
Alpha Tau Omega Chapter, Alpha Kappa Alpha Sorority, Inc.®

ESTHER- A WOMAN OF COMMUNITY AND HERITAGE

The Book of Esther

Read the Scripture:

Purpose: To illustrate God's Love and Sovereignty in any situation.

Introduction

Esther stepped up to the challenge when the existence of her family and people were severely threatened, risking her position as queen in a Persian court.

Main Characters

- Esther, a Jewish maiden turned queen,
- Mordecai her cousin and the one who raised her,
- King Xerxes and Haman, high official in the Persian court.
- Vashti, former queen

The story of Esther is rich in affirmations of how God can use an ordinary woman and move her to a position of extraordinary authority and power, if she humbles herself and is willing to walk into the position He has assigned for her.

This story is told in the entire book of Esther. It takes place in the Persian Capitol of Susa during the reign of King Xerxes (also called Ahasuerus), grandson of Cyrus the Great.

Throughout the story, the writer places emphasis on the ongoing conflict between Israel and the Amalekites. This conflict which began during the exodus (Ex 17:8-16), is one of the root causes for the brewing problem of why Mordecai will not bow to the newly appointed high ranking official in the Kings Court, named Haman.

As the book opens, the current Queen Vashti denies the King's request to parade in front of him and the men at his feast. Outraged, the king dethrones her as queen, which then requires him to look for a new queen. King Ahasuerus (uh-haz-yoo-her-russ) wanted a new wife. His helpers suggested that King Ahasuerus send for the most beautiful women of the land so that the King could choose one as his wife. One of women chosen was Esther, a young Jewish woman who grew up in the home of her cousin Mordecai. Mordecai adopted Esther when her parents died. Esther was lovely in "form and feature" (Esther 2:7).

Before Esther was sent to King Ahasuerus, she received beauty treatments for a year. Esther must have had a pleasing demeanour, as she was treated special by the man in charge of the women being groomed in the palace. When Esther was taken to King Ahasuerus, the scripture says, "he loved her more than any of the other women, therefore, he made Esther his wife". When Esther went to live at the palace of King Ahasuerus, Mordecai walked by the courtyard each day to see how Esther was doing.

When Haman, the king's advisor received a promotion from the King, he issued a mandate that "all in the land were to bow" to him (Haman). Consistently when Mordecai refused to bow to him (Esther 3:1-4), mainly since Mordecai was a Jew and refused bow to anyone except to God (Ex 20:4-5), Haman was annoyed and sought a way to kill and destroy Mordecai and all Jews (Esther 3:6). Haman devised a wicked plan to do just that (Esther 3:7-13) and tricked the king into agreeing to a law where all the Jews would be killed within twelve months (Esther 3:13). Of course, the king had no idea that Queen Esther was a Jew, or he would not have allowed this law, but Haman's deception worked.

After Esther became queen, King Ahasuerus's advisor Haman planned to kill the Jews, Esther's people. Mordecai discovered the plot and asked Esther for help. Esther was afraid. Although she was the king's wife, anyone who approached the king without the king's permission to enter his courts, could be killed. If Esther went to King Ahasuerus and he did not extend his sceptre, she could be killed. Esther needed courage to approach King Ahasuerus. Mordecai reminded Esther as she pondered going to the king's quarters (Esther 4:12-13) that *"do not think to yourself that in the king's palace you will escape any more than all the other Jews. For if you keep silent at this time, relief and deliverance will rise for the Jews from another place, but you and your father's house will perish"*.

Mordecai said to Esther (Esther 4:14b), "who knows, perhaps you have come to the kingdom for such a time as this? What a blessing when you clearly see the plan God has for your life? Knowing when to execute can be more important than the plan itself. "Esther gained strength by asking Mordecai to tell the Jews to fast and pray for three days.

On the third day, Esther got enough courage to approach King Ahasuerus. King Ahasuerus extended his sceptre to welcome her. He obviously loved Esther for more than just her beauty. He told Esther, "whatever you want, even to half of the kingdom, will be given to you." Esther's plan included inviting King Ahasuerus and Haman to a banquet.

Accordingly, King Ahasuerus and Haman went to Esther's feast. King Ahasuerus said, "Esther, whatever you seek, will be done." Esther replied, "Spare my life and my people!" King Ahasuerus was furious and asked, "Who is this with such a wicked plan would destroy you and your people? Now came the moment of truth! Who would plan such a thing?" Esther answered, "The enemy is Haman!"

King Ahasuerus gave Haman the punishment Haman had planned for Mordecai. King Ahasuerus gave Esther Haman's property, and had a law written that would protect Esther's and Mordecai's people, the Jews. The people were joyful. There was a celebration and a holiday because of Esther's courage to speak to the king.

The king gave Mordecai the signet ring which was to be given to Haman and Esther appointed Mordecai over Haman's estate. Because the edict had been given to kill the Jews, however, it could not be reversed, so the Jews were fully equipped to protect themselves and were triumphant in battle.

Points of Emphasis:

When God has chosen you, He will set a path to guide you, if you are obedient. How is this shown in this Bible Story?

- Esther was beautiful but humble in character.
- God works in mysterious ways – He can use any one for any cause, even an orphaned, Jewish woman to become Queen of Persia.
- When we put our fears to the side, God will give us the COURAGE even in moments of fear. She could have kept quiet, just hoped for the best, or turned the other way.

- Pride comes just before a fall. (Haman)
- When we please God, we can find favour even among our enemies.
- God can turn trials into triumph.
- Our prayers, voices and actions matter to God.
- God is always at work, even when our situation looks grim and uncertain.
- God's timing is always perfect; and finally, that if we plot evil for others, it can easily come back on us.

THINK ABOUT IT (DIG DEEPER):

- What are the characteristics shown by Esther that God would choose her for such a task? Could God choose you for such an assignment?
- Was Mordecai being deceitful when he told Esther to not divulge that she was a Jew? Should that have mattered?
- What danger did Esther face by going to the King's quarters?
- Do you think Mordecai was being selfish asking Esther to risk going into the Kings quarters uninvited or was he an opportunist? Is being a risktaker good or bad?
- What is the significance of Mordecai tearing his clothes and putting on sackcloth and ashes?
- What is the significance of Esther's directive to Mordecai and the Jews? Why is prayer and fasting important?
- Courage sometimes also dictate we deploy careful planning. What plan did Esther execute?
- Why do you think the King welcomed Esther uninvited? Do you see God's Hand in this? How?

- What considerations were necessary for Esther to have the courage to act? Sometimes our actions have an impact on more than just us.
- What if she was not open to the advice from Mordecai and not wise enough to plan?
- How could her relationship with Mordecai have impacted her decision? Why?
- Serving God sometimes means we may have to risk our own security. What risks did Esther take? Why do we treasure security when we know life carries no guarantees?
  - Possessions can be destroyed; beauty fades; relationships can be broken.
  - Death is inevitable.
  - Real security must be built on something beyond this life.
- Has there been a time in your life where God has made your enemy or one who meant you no good, your footstool? Can you share?
- When was the last time you made yourself available for God's use?
- What are some consequences if Esther had not acted?
- Did Esther also take risks when she trusted her maids and eunuchs? Why is important to maintain trust with your employer?

The Teaching Plan

Opening Student Involvement:

Can you think of a time when you were in the right place at the right time for God to Bless you?

Have you ever had to step up to a situation that caused you to respond to injustice? Or a time that you looked past your own safety for the benefit of others?

- Introduction to the Book of Esther – 1 of 2 Books in Bible named after a Woman
- Demonstrates God's Sovereignty and His loving care for His people
- Esther's Courageous Act that saved her people

TRUTHS OF THE STORY:
Her FAVOR- Esther 2:7-9

- Orphaned at young age.
- Raised by her cousin, Mordecai.
- "Won favour with everyone who saw her" Esther 2:9; 2:15-17.
- Her voice like music and eyes tender as a dove.
- Was of a minority race – Jews in Persia had been a minority since their deportation from Judah 100 years earlier; When God's got a blessing for you, who can stop it?

Her PLIGHT – 2:16-4:4

- Moved from poor orphaned girl to Queen of the Palace.
- Her beauty got her in, her faith kept her in.
- Found out quickly Haman was her adversary.
- Assessed the situation, including going to the King, uninvited.
- Took a risk to save her people

Her PERPETRATOR – Haman Esther 3

- Was blinded by arrogance and self-importance 3:5-6.
- Desired to control others.
- Swelled with hatred that he had no compassion in his heart –3:12-15.
- Prepared a "gallow" to murder Mordecai and all the Jews.
- His evil plot turned on him – God has an amazing way of making evil plans backfire on the perpetrator.

Her PLAN - Esther 4:4-12

- Leveraged her resources – 4:4.
- Communicated with Mordecai. Why was this significant 4:4-15?
- Settled her fear in the time of crisis 4:15.
- Determining to die for the cause 4:16-17.

Her PARTNER: Esther 6:1

- When God Spirit causes unrest
- God is working on our behalf even when we don't physically see how He's working; never forget God is working for us throughout our lives.
- Was Esther's appointment coincidence or God's Providential time? Discuss.

Her PRAISE Esther 8-9

- The King welcomed and adored Esther 5:1-7; 7:2-7.
- The Decree to Help the Jews.
- Relief in the truth being unveiled Esther 8:1-10.

Her PROFUND DELIVERANCE Esther 9-10

- God touched the King's heart. What happens when God touches you? Luke 18:35-42 –Just one touch and a blind man is healed!

- The Jews were equipped with a plan and everything they needed to defend themselves.

Your Self Examination:

I know the plans and purpose God has for my life? I will:

- _____
- _____
- _____

Esther Study ACTIVITY:

Find Words relative to this study in the Word Search Puzzle below:

Word Search

```
M S T C S L O J P D A X V D S
Z D R I B W C Q K I U V X N P
L A L B Q I F U X V H X K Y A
T M V O C N B E Y I U A D K L
C P I P B T B E P N U E E I A
T J U V Q E A N W E R S L N C
W K K H S R D P B A I T I G E
H C S X V C S I I Z S H V X D
A B P B W E J F E Q K E E E F
M W A L K D O T P N R R R R Q
A J Q K T E M V U C C X A X H
N P P N A U S G I I K E N E U
H K O F T E S R J I S Y C S T
K Y M O R D E C A I X L E H L
V M G B R I L S E E A U T H X
```

Deliverance	King Xerxes	Intercede	Obedience
Mordecai	Divine	Esther	Palace
Queen	Haman	Risk	

End with Prayer.

Notes Page:

_____
_____
_____
_____
_____
_____
_____
_____
_____
_____
_____
_____
_____
_____
_____
_____
_____
_____
_____
_____
_____
_____
_____
_____

HANNAH: A PRAYING WOMAN

Prayer is the foundational form of communication with God. When we cut out external distractions and go into full communication with God, He hears us and will often deliver us according to His Plan. Such is the case with Hannah and what I have experienced so many times in my life as Sandra and I have prayed together down through the years.

Women who fervently and passionately pray to God realize that God is the one who ultimately provides our blessings and our wellbeing. When our prayers line up with His plan, He rewards us in so many ways. I fundamentally believe that when we seek Him, acknowledge Him and accept His will for our lives, we can live more fruitful and productive lives. For we recognize that in our humility He is exalted and will answer us!

We must be careful that we do not allow external distractions deter us from a life focused on an established relationship with Him. Prayer and communication with God will unlock doors of happiness if we are willing to wait for His time and not take matters into our own hands.

Evelyn Holmes, Lifetime Friend – Gary, Indiana

HANNAH: A PRAYING WOMAN

1 Samuel 1:2 – 2:21
The Truths of the Story:

Introduction:
Have you ever made a promise to God? Did you keep your promise?

God desires women who will passionately and patiently seek Him regardless of how depressed their situation may be.

The Feast of the Tabernacle:

* Last of sacred festivals.
* Suggested completeness.
* Commemorated the Jews wilderness wandering.

The characters:

* Hannah
* Elkanah, her husband
* Peninah, Elkanah's other wife and Hannah's provoker
* Eli, The Priest

The Story:

Prayers are ***voiced*** from the perspective of our time frame; however, they are ***answered*** in God's time frame. The "give me now" mentality often causes us disappointment and disillusionment because of our impatience in waiting to see how God will bless us.

The story of Hannah demonstrates God's unyielding response to one who prayed a sincere & fervent prayer. Note that it was in God's time that she was blessed, not her own.

This story of Hannah sets the opening of the Book of 1 Samuel. The author of the book is not identified; however, it is significant that the author accentuates the importance of Samuel's birth and the effect he will have as a prophet to God's people. Hannah in her cry and petition to the Lord establishes her long-awaited son whose prophetic word and work is herald as one of the major prophets of the Old Testament. There are many truths unveiled in the first two chapters of this book.

One can see the effect of passionate prayer, enduring tribulation, and how the fulfilment of a promise made to God can turn a troubled situation into a triumphant victory. The story of Hannah demonstrates the power of a godly woman's petition and prayer to the Lord.

Hannah came to the realization that even persistent, fervent prayer is granted in God's timetable, for **she had prayed many, many years** to have a son, yet God had not responded to her. I Samuel 1:5 pens '*...the Lord had closed her womb*'. The Lord seeks pure and passionate hearts that will surrender to Him. Hannah did not give up, but prayed 'earnestly' to the Lord, vowing that if He blessed her with a son, she would give the child back to him, 1 Samuel 1:11.

The Jewish custom mandated that each year, the man and his household would pay homage to the Lord at the Feast of the Tabernacle, the last of the sacred festivals commemorating the completion of the harvest of the Israelites wandering in the wilderness. It was a happy and joyous celebration. Refer to Leviticus 23:33-43 for more detail on the feast of the tabernacle.

Even though for most, it was a happy and joyous occasion, no doubt Hannah had to emotionally prepare herself for this "celebration". Year after year, she was provoked by Elkanah's other wife, which made her feel unusually unworthy because she had no children.

Have you ever been on an emotional roller coaster, where it seems life's ups just seem to pull you down? I'm sure this is how Hannah must have felt as noted in the Scripture, *"O Lord Almighty, if you will only look upon your servant's misery and remember me"*, 1 Sam 1: 11, NIV.

The Scripture does not tell us HOW the marriage to Penninah and Elkanah came about. Was it Hannah's decision, like Sarah's in times past to provide a mistress for her husband? Was it simply because of the culture where it was legal for a man to have multiple wives? We don't know. We do know, however, that Elkanah loved Hannah, which is demonstrated by the fact that he would give her a double portion of blessings at the time of offering. 1Samuel 1:3 -4 state, *Year after year this man went up from his town to worship and sacrifice to the Lord Almighty at Shiloh…*

Whenever the day came for Elkanah to sacrifice, he would give portions of the meat for his wife Penninah and all her sons and daughters. But to Hannah he gave a double portion because he loved her" NIV.

No doubt, Hannah could have retaliated, as her husband Elkanah's other wife Peninah chided and provoked her year after year because she was barren. Certainly, Hannah could have retaliated, as she was reprimanded and provoked her year after year because **'the Lord had closed her womb'.** In other words, she was barren, without child. Instead of demonstrating evil behavior, Hannah demonstrated godly character and communed with the ONLY one who could change her crisis into a celebration! She prayed so passionately that the priest Eli, thought she was drunken with wine. Verse 15 states, *not so my lord, Hannah replied, I am a woman who is deeply troubled. I have not been drinking"* NIV. Have you ever been so overtaken by the Holy Spirit that you feel God's presence all over you?

She **prayed** and **wept** much knowing that God was the ONLY one who could change her circumstance into a celebration! Hannah made a vow that if he would 'look upon thy servant's misery and remember me, and forget not your servant, but remember her and give her a son, then I will give him to the Lord for all the days of his life' 1Sam 1:11. The Lord heard Hannah's cry and blessed her with a son. Being the devoted woman, she was, she upheld her commitment to God, and so when her son Samuel was born, she dedicated him to the Lord.

Have you ever made a promise to God? Lord if you…, then I will…. Did you fulfil your promise? Unlike many of us, Hannah fulfilled her promise. Such joy must have overcome her to know that she was finally going to have a son. Hannah's crisis was truly turned into a celebration.

In today's study, we are provided a stellar example of a woman whose impeccable character deals with a familiar crisis and passionate cry to the Lord led her to an ultimate BLESSED commemoration.

Hannah's Crisis
Have you ever been in an uncomfortable situation? You want to run and hide, but you can't escape the situation?

Hannah's Character
How can Christian character make a difference when you are in the middle of a crisis?
- Praying Woman – Jeremiah 29:12
- Patient Woman – Romans 12:12
- Painful Woman – Psalm 37: 1
- Personal Worship – Psalms 95:6

Hannah's Cry
Hannah's Cry –v. 9-15 Have you ever been so overtaken by the Holy Spirit that you feel God's presence all around you?
- Wept much & prayed to the Lord.
- Psalm 40:1 – 'I waited patiently for the Lord; he turned to me and heard my cry.
- Finding consolation for women of 'sorrowful' spirit.

Hannah's Creed
Have you ever made a promise to God? Lord if you…, then I will….
Did you fulfil your promise?
- Psalm 119:58

- Her follow through on commitment
- Her child's dedication

Hannah's Celebration:
Can you think about a time you celebrated after a long-awaited prayer is answered?
- Review Hannah's Song of Praise
- **Psalm 34:1**

How can you find peace in persecution?

Pray - seek God's Plan
Engage your heart
Abandon selfish ambition
Consecrate yourself
Endow your mind with focus

The Teaching Plan – Hannah

The story of Hannah demonstrates God' s unyielding response to one who prayed a sincere & fervent prayer. However, it was in God's timeframe that she was blessed, not her own.

Opening Student Involvement:
Questions to Ponder—

Think about a time in your life where you had to depend solely upon God? Did God come through for you?

Lord, if you _____then, I

_____.

Her Character – Proverbs 12:4 - Maintains her example of Christian womanhood

- *Praying woman* - *"Evening, and morning, and at noon, will I pray, and cry aloud: and he shall hear my voice."* Psalm 55:17
  "Pray without ceasing." 1 Thessalonians 5:17
- *Patient woman* – Romans 12:12 (NIV) 12 Be joyful in hope, patient in affliction, faithful in prayer.
- *Provoked woman* - Ephesians 4:31 (ESV) Let all bitterness and wrath and anger and clamour and slander be put away from you, along with all malice.
- *Painful woman* - Philippians 4:6-7 – Be careful for nothing; but in everything by prayer and supplication with thanksgiving let your requests be made known unto God
- *Personal worshipping woman* - Jeremiah 20:13. 13 Sing to the LORD! Give praise to the LORD!

Her Crisis – v. 4-8; I Corinthians 12:7-10

- Relationship with Elkanah – barren
- Rivalry with Peninah
- Respect for her situation

Her Cry – v. 9-15 Psalm 40:1

- "Wept much & prayed to the Lord.
- Woman of sorrowful spirit.
- Whole being c aught into the Spirit of the Lord.

Her Creed - v. 11 Psalm 119:49, 58

- Lord if you… then
- Her follow through on her commitment.
- Her child's dedication v. 24-28

Her Celebration - Chapter 2:1-10

- **P** ray and seek the Father's plan
- **E** ngage with your heart
- **A** bandon selfish ambitions
- **C** onsecrate yourself to walk in grace
- **E** ndow your mind with focus

Meditate on Psalm 40

Hannah

```
J  I  N  I  K  X  T  H  F  I  D  U  X  W  E  P  E
P  E  M  L  R  P  B  Z  R  T  E  L  K  A  N  A  H
M  A  O  G  Q  R  Z  F  T  E  S  I  M  O  R  P  Y
B  L  T  C  O  P  I  H  E  R  P  L  G  W  O  X  T
M  A  S  I  S  K  Q  T  P  B  K  R  S  F  J  S  R
O  V  U  H  E  C  A  E  A  V  D  E  A  X  P  H  R
W  I  C  P  R  N  A  L  W  T  R  M  Z  Y  X  H  A
D  T  H  R  O  C  T  M  E  V  E  N  F  G  E  B  D
E  S  S  I  E  W  U  W  A  M  X  O  A  N  M  R  O
S  E  I  E  N  O  X  N  O  Z  O  P  T  G  G  P  U
O  F  W  S  Y  S  T  N  X  M  Y  P  C  H  L  M  C
L  M  E  T  K  C  S  K  B  H  A  Q  V  I  E  M  M
C  E  J  M  B  H  A  N  N  A  H  N  T  O  C  R  D
D  E  D  I  C  A  T  I  O  N  H  P  V  O  G  S  S
N  Z  K  B  D  E  L  H  M  N  E  K  H  H  C  K  S
I  T  R  L  T  F  R  C  J  W  Y  D  C  O  D  E  C
E  R  E  T  C  A  R  A  H  C  P  S  A  M  U  E  L
```

Peace   Dedication   Promise   Prayer   Jewish Custom   Irritate Others   Character
Patient Woman   Wept   Closed Womb   Servant   Festival   Elkanah   Priest
Samuel   Hannah

Notes Pages:

Becoming a Successful Businesswoman
BUSINESS 101

Success isn't just about what you accomplish in your life; it's about what you inspire others to do." —Unknown

In today's fast paced, highly competitive, and evolving world, it is more important than ever to maintain high moral standards and ethics in the workplace. Attracting and developing a high performing team that embraces and embodies the company's core values is critical to carrying out the company's mission and achieving success in today's global economy. Respect for the individual, high employee engagement and strong business acumen must be the fibre for high achieving, exemplary organizations.

No matter what your business or the position you hold, establishing strong relationships within the organization is key to fostering an atmosphere of teamwork and unified purpose. One of the most important lessons I learned early on in my career, was that relationships mattered as much as the actual business outcomes. Fostering a collaborative environment based on mutual respect (despite differences) yielded far better results once I figured this out.

As a leader, it is important that your team is motivated by your clearly articulated vision and that they understand and embrace the goals of the organization.

Each person plays a pivotal role in the overall success of the organization and leaders must set the bar high and ensure team members understand how they fit into this equation. By maintaining value-based principles, you can create a culture of success and an atmosphere for overachievement.

I challenge any woman who wants to succeed as a businesswoman, to adapt these principles and take to heart the old adage "do unto others as you would have them do unto you."

Melinda Chausse
Sandra's former manager and Financial Services
Industry Executive

LYDIA
A FAITHFUL BUSINESSWOMAN

Lydia of Thyatira
Acts 16: 11-15; 40
Read the Scripture
Points of Emphasis: Introduction:

God will intentionally find the women He needs to provide the service and hospitality needed to motivate his people.

Setting:

Paul and Silas is on their 2nd missionary journey, when God directs them to go to Thyatira. When they get there, they are puzzled because there is no synagogue or central place of worship. What they find is a group of women on the outskirts of town, down by the riverside having a prayer meeting. They meet Lydia, the prayer meeting leader. Lydia was a businesswoman who was a "worshipper" v.14 of God.

Main Characters:

- Lydia, a businesswoman of purple clothing
- Paul, Silas and Timothy on a missionary journey
- Women of Thyatira

The Story:

Nestled in the 16th chapter of Acts is another beautiful and obscure woman of the Bible. In fact, we glean so many truths about her from just 2 short passages of scripture:

Acts 16:13-15 English Standard Version (ESV)

13And on the <u>Sabbath day</u> we went <u>outside the gate</u> to <u>the riverside</u>, where <u>we supposed there was a place of prayer</u>, and we sat down and <u>spoke to the women</u> who had come together. 14One who heard us was a woman named <u>Lydia</u>, from the <u>city of Thyatira</u>, a <u>seller of purple goods</u>, who was a <u>worshiper of God. The Lord opened her heart</u> to <u>pay attention</u> to what was said by Paul. 15And after <u>she was baptized</u>, and <u>her household as well</u>, she urged us, saying, "If you have <u>judged me to be faithful</u> to the Lord, <u>come to my house</u> and <u>stay."</u> And she <u>prevailed upon us</u>. Wow! So much to unpack in these short two verses which sets a sure model for women who are in the workplace. We get several insights from this passage. Let's explore.

Although today many put their careers, jobs and chores ahead of God, Lydia set aside time to pray and worship God. I find this so interesting because Lydia was a Gentile, so she would not necessarily be familiar with the worship and legendary history as a Jew would. The scripture does not say how she developed her relationship or desire to reverence God. It is however one of the key attributes given to her in these two short verses.

On the Sabbath day, Lydia and a few other women went outside the gate to the riverside to pray. One might ask, why did they go outside the gate and why didn't they go into the synagogue. A couple points to note here. In order to have a synagogue (church) in those times, you had to have 10 Jewish men and a rabbi. Interestingly there were few Jews in Philippi and it was customary since there was no synagogue to assemble near running water to pray.

Thyatira, a small province of Asia was famous for dyeing works, especially royal purple fabrics. Lydia was a successful businesswoman who followed the moral teachings of the scripture. She had not however been truly converted in the understanding of who Jesus is or Judaism. When Paul found Lydia and the women praying, he and his fellow companions joined them. This points very clearly a difference in Paul's earlier position in accepting and worshipping with women.

As Paul preached, the scripture says Lydia's "heart was opened" as she paid attention to the Word and she responded to the gospel message, asking to be baptized. Not only her, but her entire household. The scripture does not tell us who made up Lydia's household. One can assume with her success and status she had a staff of workers and employees who were respectful of her. It did not take much for Lydia to understand that baptism is needed to be included in God's family.

Jesus commanded "go and make disciples of all the nations, baptizing them in the name of the Father and the Son and Holy spirit. It is with this conviction that Lydia on this day was baptized. A woman who is to be a successful businesswoman must demonstrate certain character traits. Integrity and honesty are two that readily come to mind for me.

Having spent 39 years as a businesswoman, I cannot over emphasize the importance of respect, integrity and high moral standards in the workplace. As I walked into my purpose of being a successful sales and marketing executive, certain principles became apparent to me and is so needed if you are to succeed or walk fully into your purpose. Do you know God's purpose in your life? Can you be as confident, certain and positive as Lydia was?

"It is in Christ that we find our who we are and what we are living for. Long before we heard of Christ..., He had his eye on us, had designs for glorious living; part of the overall purpose he is working out in everything and everyone. Ephesians 1:11 MSG.

Undoubtedly, Lydia through her worship of God and recognizing the importance of worshipping him was glorified as she heard the good news of salvation and the Love of Jesus. While she had recognized God as her creator 'father', she now understood Jesus as her loving and sacrificial saviour.

As a result, Lydia's gift of hospitality manifest itself, asking the men to stay with her. She not only opened her heart to hear, but she also opened her home. Obviously given her status in the community and the successfulness of her business, Lydia enjoyed the comforts of the time. Lydia insisted that Paul and Silas stay with her.

Her home was probably one of the nicer homes in Thyatira and she looked forward to entertaining these messengers of God. She willingly shared what she had and it appears demonstrated her gift of hospitality so well that when they were returning after being in prison, cast out demons, converted a jailer and shook the prison with prayer, they wanted to go back to Lydia's house. Do people look forward to coming to your house and fellowshipping with you?

Becoming a woman God can use in the workplace, requires we use some of Lydia's character traits. She was:

- Woman with business ethics and judgement.
- Woman of faith – acknowledged God and worshipped Him.
- Woman who leveraged resources – although no formal synagogue, she gathered her team and prayed down by the riverbanks. Worship was important to her.
- Woman of influence – her whole household followed her and were baptized.
- Woman of Persuasion – she insisted that Paul and Silas stay and get refreshed at her house.
- Woman of hospitality – she was not selfish and used her blessings to be a blessing to others

Lydia was a woman who God blessed with business savvy, resources and intellect. She was open to having a deeper relationship with God and in doing so she was blessed, her house was blessed, and the men of God were blessed.

Are you a businesswoman? A woman leader? A mission leader?

How can Lydia's character be a model for you?

Points of Emphasis:

Introduction:

•   There was no synagogue or church for Lydia to worship, but she found a way to praise and pray to God.

•   Lydia was a worshipper before she was introduced to Jesus.

•   Thyatira was a trade port and specialized in manufacturing fine cloths of purple.

•   Lydia was a businesswoman, obviously with a good reputation.

•   How can her example be a footprint for women in business today?

•   Had a special heart that was ready to be used by God as a vessel of honour.

THINK ABOUT IT!

•   Why did the writer emphasize the sabbath? What do you recall about the sabbath growing up?

•   Dig deeper to understand why there was not a synagogue in Philippi. Jewish law required 10 men plus a rabbi to establish a synagogue.

•   Lydia was regarded as the first documented convert to Christianity in Europe. Interesting since women were not highly regarded during this time. What insights can you glean from this?

•   Why was Lydia's baptism of significance?

•   What does it mean to be converted or what is the conversion process?

•   What are characteristics of the "gift" of Hospitality?

- Discuss faith.

The Teaching Plan

Can you be a Christian and a successful business woman? In what ways?

What are some Christian values that can be demonstrated although many times you cannot discuss religion in the workplace?

In this lesson, we study a woman who gives us a good roadmap for being a woman of God in her place of work. In this case she was a successful businesswoman. The example she provides and the principles she exemplifies apply to any profession or area of business. Lydia shows:

- Reverence and the importance of praying and worshipping God.
- She had a willing heart to hear God's word.
- God's word convicts us and calls us to action.
- Obedience to God's word and causes an exciting response.
- Baptism is the outward recognition that we have accepted Christ and want a higher level of relationship with Him.
- Her household respected her and followed her actions to be baptized.
- Hospitality makes a difference in building relationships.

Lydia's Fortune – *"But seek ye first the kingdom of God and His righteousness and all things will be given to you. Matthew 6:33.*

During this time, **Purple cloth** was valuable and very expensive. It's value was equated with that of silver. It was usually a sign of royalty and nobility.

- Successful Businesswoman- *Dealer of Purple*
- Well known in the city,
- Obviously, she lived well. Enough room for her "household" which suggests her servants lived with her and Paul and Silas were also invited to stay until they left for the furtherance of their journey.

- **Food for Thought**: Why did God change Paul and Silas' direction and send them to Thyatira? Do you think God knows when we need to further our relationship with Him? How do you recognize when God is sending you a message or messenger?

Lydia's Formula – *that if you confess with your mouth the Lord Jesus and believe in your heart that God has raised Him from the dead, you will be saved.* ***Romans 10:9-10 NKJV***
Plan of Salvation

- ABC's of Salvation: A= Accept B= Believe C= Confess
What do you remember about your baptism?
If you have not been baptized, consider accepting Jesus as Lord (Ruler) in your life.
Consider sharing the plan of salvation with others. It's as easy as ABC.

Lydia's Faith – "So faith comes by hearing and hearing the Word of God. Romans 10:17.

The dictionary defines faith as "strong belief in God or in the doctrines of a religion, based on spiritual apprehension rather than proof"

- What is it and how do you grow in it?
- The scripture says God gives faith. Ask God to increase your **faith**. If you are struggling in your **faith**, ask God for more of it.
- Obedience. Focus on obeying God.
- Spend time reading and hearing God's word – 2 Timothy 2:15
- Spend time with other believers. We are meant to worship – Hebrews 10:25.

Lydia's Family – *How good and pleasant it is when God's people live together in unity!" – Psalm 133:1*

- Not much is said about her family. We can surmise that her household respected her since all believed and were baptized with her.
- Why is it important that we worship together as a family.
- Do you agree that "a family who prays together, stays together"?

Lydia's Friendship –
- A model of Service and Hospitality.
- Lydia demonstrated her hospitality toward Paul and Silas by insisting that they stay at her house.
- Lydia left such an impression that Paul and Silas returned to visit her.
- Would you say you have an inviting spirit? In what ways?
- Lydia not only opened her heart; she opened her home

Activity:

Sing as Song of Fellowship with your Study Group.

What a Fellowship (lyrics)
What a fellowship, what a joy divine,

Leaning on the everlasting arms;

What a blessedness, what a peace is mine,

Leaning on the everlasting arms.

Refrain

Leaning, leaning, safe and secure from all alarms;

Leaning, leaning, leaning on the everlasting arms.

O how sweet to walk in this pilgrim way,

Leaning on the everlasting arms;

O how bright the path grows from day to day, Leaning
on the everlasting arms.

Refrain

What have I to dread, what have I to fear,

Leaning on the everlasting arms;

I have blessed peace with my Lord so near,

Leaning on the everlasting arms?

End in prayer.

Notes Page:

Study Activity:

Match the definition with the Word

1. Home City   A. Synagogue

2. Businesswoman   B. Paul

3. Delivered God's Word   C. Philippi

4. Was baptized with Lydia   D. Faith

5. Colour of Fabric   E. Lydia

6. When courtesy is shown   F. Thyatira

7. Believe when you don't see   G. Household

8. Need 10 Jewish Men and Rabbi   H. Hospitality
   to form

9. Where Lydia lived   I. Baptism

10. Outward expression of belief   J. Purple

TRUE FRIENDSHIP IS A BLESSING

"One who has unreliable friends soon comes to ruin, but there is a friend who sticks closer than a brother." Proverbs 18:24

Aspire to be the kind of friend you want as a friend, a Christ-Centered Friend. One who seeks to walk in the spirit; one who understands who they are in Christ; one who knows the love of Christ and loves Christ as their saviour; one who seeks to grow in Christ and, one who accepts themselves and others exactly as they are while growing in HIS grace.

True friendship is self-giving. I find true friendship in Sandra Reese Jolla and want to parallel our friendship to Ruth's and Naomi's. Sandra (Ruth) is blessed with generosity, compassion and the spirit of Christ. Randi (Naomi), understands, Sandra's love for her and Sandra's love of God (they are both fiercely loyal to one another). Their friendship and love for each other continues to blossom to this day and will forever more. We help each other through our trials in life and celebrate each other's blessings (Sandra's God is my God and we journey together); we understand the beautiful image of Christ's love for us. Sandra and I embrace each other's differences and appreciate God's individual purpose for our life (true friendship breaks boundaries). I'm blessed to be Sandra's oldest daughter's godmother ("your people shall be my people"). Our friendship demonstrates our shared love of Christ and our love for each other as we walk together through life in God's grace. What kind of friend are you?

Randi Miles – former co-worker and lifetime friend-
Denver, Colorado

NAOMI AND RUTH – A MODEL OF TRUE FRIENDSHIP

The Story of Ruth and Naomi From Tragedy to Triumph Ruth The Truths of the Story:

Introduction:
What are the characteristics of a 'true' friend?
* Loyalty
* Devotion
* Respect
* Trust
* Compassion

The Book of Ruth:

* Moab- foreigner; foreign country.
* Importance of faithful love in human relationship.
* The time of judges & national disunity.

Naomi's family:

* Elimelech, her husband
* Mahillon, her son
* Chillon, her son; Talk about the importance of:
* Family
* Ruth, her daughter-in-law
* Orpah, her daughter-in-law

Sometimes life can get **dark** and **dreary**. How can we maintain hope during this darkness?

The Story:

True friendship is established through a combination of good times, and bad times, through trials and triumphs. It is made stronger in times of weakness and accelerates to higher heights good times. The book of Ruth embodies this truth and epitomizes the bond of **relationship, friendship and sisterhood.**

The book is a tender account of a gentile woman from Moab named Ruth, and her friendship with a Hebrew woman from Bethlehem named Naomi. It is a story fraught with kindness and faithfulness, a tale of integrity, hardship and blessings. It is a story that clearly demonstrates how sincere **devotion** and **dedication**, even amid troubling times can lead to ultimate **delight.**

The story is set in the time of the judges, a time characterized with religious and moral degeneracy, national disunity and frequent foreign opposition. Ruth 1:1 states *"In the days when judges ruled, there was famine in the land, and a man from Bethlehem in Judah together with his wife and two sons, went to live in the country of Moab".*

In our text, we find that Naomi's husband, had to leave his home which was Bethlehem of **Judah**—the **city of bread** because there was no food in the land. Because there was a famine, food was scarce, and there were no jobs. It was a **Dark and Dreary** time!

Because of a desire to live and to provide for him, his wife, and his two sons— Mahillon and Chillon. Elimelech is forced to leave his home and go to the land of Moab. Moab is in a foreign country, but at least they are together as a family. It is a place where the Moabites do not like them, and they do not like the Moabites.

Dark and Dreary! Can you imagine the challenges just to get established in this foreign land?

> **Shortly after leaving their home,** Naomi's Son's marry two foreign girls by the name of Orpah and Ruth. Shortly after arriving in Moab, Naomi's husband, Elimelech dies.
>
> **Dark and Dreary!** Three years after this, both of Naomi's son's die and Naomi is left with nothing but her two Daughter's-in- law, Orpah and Ruth.
>
> **Dark and Dreary!**
> The scripture says, *"Naomi was left without her two sons and her husband". Naomi and her two daughters-in law head back home to the land of Judah.*
>
> Desolate and despondent, Naomi encourages her daughters-in law to return to Moab. Losing a loved one can be devastating, losing three within three years, is overwhelming.
>
> Can you imagine how Naomi must have felt? Have you lost a dear family member? Can you imagine losing your husband and two sons within three years?
>
> Naomi was so destitute, she insists on changing her name from Naomi, which means joy to Mara, meaning bitter because the Lord had dealt with her bitterly.

In our times of trouble, God will send persons in our lives to make us stronger; to serve as lampposts for us when our lights are dim, and our paths seem weary. Such is the case **with Ruth. Although Orpah follows Naomi's urging to go** back to Moab, Ruth clings to her mother-in-law, replying, *"don't urge me to leave you, or turn back from you. Where you go, I will go, and where you stay, I will stay. Your people will be my people and your God my God.* The Lord always has a 'ram in the bush'. Even when we are not sure how we will provide the 'sacrifice', the Lord makes a way. Thank God for the Ruth's in our lives who stick with us to help us make it through. Ecclesiastes 4:9, *states, two are better than one, because they have a good reward for their labour.*

What was it about Naomi that made Ruth cling to her? How do your daughters-in law or sons-in law view you? Would they cleave or leave? Did Ruth need Naomi, or did Naomi need Ruth? Maybe they needed each other.

They returned home after the cold and wintry days of their lives. Not just the winter of the season, but Naomi and Ruth have had some cold-wintry days in their lives. **They have had some DARK AND DREARY DAYS—** Naomi has lost her husband, and her two sons; Ruth has lost her husband, and here they are two widows, depending on the Lord and the Land to provide for them.

Lois Evans in her book, "**Seasons of a Woman's Life**" states "that even in our dark seasons, we must not forget who you are and to whom you belong. You must praise amid pain. God still has a plan and a purpose for our lives."

Describe Naomi's disposition:

- Depressed
- Desolate
- Despondent

Can you imagine how she must have felt?

How is Ruth's disposition different from Naomi's?

- Compassionate
- Caring
- Considerate
- Costly

How would others define your disposition?

How have you responded when dark and dreary days have come upon you?

We should always remember There is always a BRIGHTER day ahead!

PRAISING GOD THROUGH THE PAIN.
REALIZING OUR PURPOSE

Together, Naomi and Ruth return to Bethlehem. Naomi's spirits low, feeling afflicted and defeated. Perhaps the support from Ruth provided her the power to sustain her through the disbelief of the town folk. The scripture reveals in Chapter 1 of Ruth, verse 19-20 — *'the whole town was stirred because of them, and the women exclaimed, can that be Naomi? Don't call me Naomi...I went away full, but the Lord has brought me back empty.*

What do you do when your life seems to have turned for the worse? When misfortune strikes, how can we look for good in a seemingly bad situation? God knows what we are going through. He sends people in our lives to sustain us, even when we are ready to give up. The heart is happiest when it beats for others. Ruth moves from **a foreign provincial** to the **sole provider.** She did not let pride and position interfere with her purpose.

It just so happens that Elimelech had a relative, Boaz, "a mighty man of wealth," One who not only had a good reputation, but he had servants, hand maidens, and he **also had some money**— **tell me what God won't do!** Boaz owned fields and had many workers.

It was customary for the men to cut the grain and for the female servants to go behind them to bind the grain in sheaves. Ruth gleaned what was **left** from that -- the leftovers of the leftovers! Samuel 2:7 – *"Please let me glean and gather among the sheaves, behind the harvesters"*, Ruth asks.

Ruth and Naomi's winter season is about to turn into spring. Notice that when they return, it is springtime! As women, we go through seasons in our lives, we must be assured that 'weeping only endures for a night; JOY comes in the morning'!

Notice also, that nowhere does the scripture say she complained to God about Naomi's and her plight. She decided to do something about her situation. The scripture show that she was 'faithful' and had worked in the field from morning until evening. God is looking for women who will humble themselves and be guided by love and loyalty and who will find a way out of no way.

Ruth was on a mission, and because of her piety, she is noticed by King Boaz, as she gleans in the fields. **Divine providence** is about to make **purposeful provisions** for Ruth and Naomi. God will take care of you, no matter what life deals you. **Boaz, wealthy**-Ruth Poor; **Boaz, Israelite,** Ruth a Moabite; **Boaz is Old,** Ruth is young— Nothing but God's grace! Notice also, that Ruth didn't go looking for Boaz. Her quiet, calm and hard-working spirit drew him to her. As single ladies, we must stop looking for Boaz and let Boaz find you! Be busy about doing the master's work.

This story provides an example of how God can bless us through our burdens, if we are faithful and focused. Ruth, a woman of noble character as described in verse 3:10, wins the heart of Boaz the king. Proverbs 31:10 states *"Who can find a woman of noble character, her worth is far more than rubies." NIV*.

Ruth and Naomi went from **Trial to Triumph.** Christian maturity is manifest through the tests and trials life brings our way. Weeping may endure for a day, But JOY comes. Trials and suffering for the Kingdom's sake is worth more than it costs.

Why is friendship important? Jesus wants to be our friend. What traits do you look for in a friend?

Ruth's Actions:

- She wanted to be Purposeful.
- She sought Protection.
- She became a Provider.

How can you have joy amid pain?

Seasons come and go in a Woman's Life. What season are you in today? Summer, hot and sizzling; fall – moving in into a new place; winter – shut up and uncertain or Summer – happy and joyous!

The GOOD NEWS from Ruth and Naomi – JOY comes in the morning. Make the best of a bad situation…don't complain. Divine Providence is when God steps in and takes control of your situation. You don't know how it happened or when it happened.

Just always remember "What God has for me" …it is for me! Boaz gives Ruth the ultimate compliment when he describes her as having 'noble character'.

How would your husband characterize you? Why do we go looking for "Boaz"? How can my character draw "Boaz" to me?

The Lord is looking for women who will stand during adversity. Having faith when all else fails.

True friendship is established through good times, and bad times, trials and triumphs. It is made stronger in times of weakness and accelerates to higher heights during good times. The book of Ruth embodies this truth and epitomizes the bond of relationship, friendship and sisterhood.

Think of a time when you felt most alone?

Think of a time when you felt the most cared for?

Both extremes are exemplified in the story of Ruth and Naomi

Consider and discuss the **characteristics** of a 'true' friend?

- Loyalty
- Devotion
- Respect
- Trust
- Compassion

Contrast Ruth and Naomi's dispositions:

Naomi: Matthew 11:28-30

Ruth: Philippians 4:13; Galatians 5:22-23

- Moral Integrity
- Acts of kindness
- Provider
- Humility
- Loyalty

Which disposition best characterizes **YOUR** style?

Ruth's Actions:

- Purposeful
- Protection
- Provider

How can you have **joy** amidst **pain**?
Think about this equation:

J esus 1st
O thers 2nd
Y ou LAST!

Notes Page:

A MOTHER'S LOVE

In Loving Memory of my mother
Mrs. Gloria Grant Reese Philpot

Deeper than the roots of an old oak tree and wider than the widest part of the ocean is what I envision when I think about a mother's love. The joy, nourishment, sacrifice, and motivation that only a mother can give comes readily to mind when I think about my mother's love.

There was nothing that my mother had me to believe I could not do! "The sky is the limit" I heard her say so many times during my formidable years. Although there were times, I felt challenged and questioned if I could go on, but my mother would propel me like an eagle dropping her baby for its first flight. Little did I know at that time, that a little risk yields a lot of rewards. Mothers know no boundaries when the lives of their children are threatened. Such is the case with Rizpah. Although a concubine of Saul, the meaning of this story is so much deeper than how her children got here. It demonstrates the sheer essence of a mother who would go to no end to demonstrate her genuine love for her children.

A mother's love, that wonderfully designed special package from heaven is filled with God's special love and special care and is like none other. A mother's love reminds me of the love that Christ has for us in that it is unconditional, forever, and eternal.

Sandra Reese Jolla – Author
In remembrance of my mother!

RIZPAH – A MOTHER'S LOVE

Scripture:

2 Samuel 21

Read the Scripture:

Introduction:

Has there ever been a time in your life where your world within minutes turned from Triumph to Tragedy?

Such is the case with this story. Rizpah, one of Saul's concubines is on top of the world enjoying life, even as a mistress, with full access to her palace living quarters and servants at her beckoning call, until she received news that her two sons, because they were of Saul's seed had been destined to be hung. What fear, what terror this mother must have felt at this unfortunate time?

The setting: 2 Samuel 21:1-6

King David summons God to inquire of the 3-year famine in the land and is informed it is because of the broken covenant between Saul and the Gibeonites. King David, wanting to make amends with the Gibeonites for Saul's earlier attack on their people, summons the Gibeonites. He offers land, gold, and many other amenities.

They refused them all and only wanted any remaining 'seeds' of Saul to be killed. That included Rizpah's 2 sons and 5 of sons of Saul's daughter. Jonathan, also Saul's son was spared because of an oath he and David had sworn before the Lord.

The Characters:

- Rizpah, one of Saul's concubines and mother of 2 of his sons
- David, newly appointed King of Israel.
- Gibeonites – native remnant of the Amorites-the people in possession of the promised land when the Israelites took possession of the land; and the people Joshua had promised they could stay in the land.

Nestled in the scripture of 2 Samuel 21 is a story of a woman whose love for her children led her to risk her life in a battle of ravenous ravens who wanted to eat her son's flesh. Although not a lengthy story, and a woman of almost no significance in the grand scheme of major Bible Stories, is this woman Rizpah. The fact that she was a concubine of Saul's had little relevance when the call came for her to demonstrate love for her children.

Because of her endurance and profound steps to protect her children, I felt it worthy to lift her story in the chronicles of Victorious women. In God's eyes, position, prestige and power don't really matter. Only your vigilance, sacrifice and sometimes risks that demonstrate your faithfulness is all that matters to God. Perseverance with profound hope yields deliverance.

Rizpah had two sons by Saul. This story takes place after Saul's death and David's early reign as King of Israel. During David's reign, he reaches out to the Gibeonites to try to restore the covenant made between Joshua and the Gibeonites (Joshua) which Saul had broken by killing many, many Gibeonites. The only restitution the Gibeonites would agree to is to have ALL descendants of Saul hung. This of course would include Rizpah's two sons – Armoni and Mephibosheth.

How quickly our lives can change. Even as a concubine, Rizpah enjoyed many of the benefits awarded a mistress of the king. She lived well, had maidservants and lived a charming life until she received word that her sons along with 5 of Saul's other sons were to be hung, not necessarily through any fought of theirs, but because of Saul's lack of commitment to the covenant given many years before.

What do you do when your life suddenly turns from triumph to tragedy? What could she do? Here she is a mother who is facing execution of her sons and there is nothing she can do.

On top of that, God caused a famine in the land for three years. When David suspects the famine is of divine intervention, he asks God and God confirms that the famine is truly punishment for Saul's massacre some 40 years earlier of the Gibeonites who had been protected by treaty since Israel first entered the Promise Land. David complies with the Gibeonites' demand in taking the seven remaining sons and grandsons of Saul.

After the executions, Rizpah stood guard over the slain bodies of her sons and five others. What a difference a day makes. This woman of extraordinary strength, determination, and hope found herself trapped in an inescapable situation. What do you do when you feel so helpless, in despair with no one to call upon? When you find yourself in a conflict between what is and what ought to be?

Rizpah stripped herself of title and position, took sack cloth to cover a rock, and with a stick; she fought off Ravens during the day and wild beasts at night to keep them from eating her son's flesh. Day after day, she stood in defence of the wild as she protected her sons' bodies and flesh.

Can you imagine for 4-5 months the sense of despair as she wailed at the beasts to go away? People passing daily shaking their heads thinking she was a lunatic to continue to fight when obviously the flesh which was once on her sons had turned to bones. The stench which had to cover the air as she remembered the wholesome life she and her sons had shared. Her love for her sons was far stronger than the stench and decay she was forced to witness.

What lessons can this obscure woman in the Bible share with us as she took everything in her to protect the remains of her sons. This story reminds me of the extent of a mother's love and what she will sacrifice to ensure the wellbeing of her children.

In many respects it helped me to recall my mother and how hard she worked to provide for us to have a decent and wholesome life as she was determined to move us out of government assisted living to a home of our own. She faced difficulty, defeat, and sometime disgust as she continuously worked from every angle possible to provide and protect us from a threatening and violent environment of the "projects". She too held on to her faith and hope in God calling upon His unfailing love.

Because of someone else's actions, she finds herself as the only catalyst at this strange time of grief and loss. As she waved off threat after threat, I can imagine the thoughts that must have run through her mind. How long will this last? How can I at least get a decent burial for my boys? Who will hear my cry and will answer me? What did I do to deserve such punishment? Lord, Hear my cry!

This story clearly demonstrates a mother's love and what she is willing to do to protect her children. Much like God looks after and provides for us and assures us in Psalm 23. He is our shepherd and looks after us even when we walk through the "valley of the shadow of death". His rod and His staff they comfort us. Surely, she had no idea when she was enjoying such a life of luxury in the palace that such a day would come for her, but she never wavered. Like we never know what ball life will throw us. Although friends tried to persuade her to leave, she was resilient, patient and a survivor.

She had watched her sons be slaughtered like animals and then had to witness and watch them as life left their bodies, the change in color of their skin as life slowly dissipated and they became bones. Days passed, then weeks, then months. She had to be tired and sleepy, limp less and weak, hot sun during the day and then cold frail nights. But the love of her children kept her going.

How would you have handled this? She watched her dreams, vision and her children die on that mountain as passer-by's mocked, starred and thought she was crazy. She trusted that God would one day intercede and give her sons a proper burial. And sure enough, soon after the deaths, King David was asked to remember her.

It is amazing how God shows up just when we are about to give up. David remembered and ordered to have all of them be given a proper burial. The triumphant JOY that must have thrilled Rizpah's heart.

Look at how God not only delivered her, but how he protected her even when she thought she was alone. No hurt or harm came to her after such a long and treacherous experience. A mother EXTRAORDINAIRE! Nothing or no one could turn her from the love of her children. Amazing isn't it that is how this parallels to how God cares for us as His children?

Rizpah's Reckoning & Sense of Discernment: -
the discerning heart seeks knowledge. Proverbs 15:14

A woman called of God stays intimately connected with God and keeps a discerning heart. God will grant her discernment for and about her children, regardless of the situation she and her children may find themselves.

What do you do when faced with a calamity?

What would you, as a mother have done when faced with such news?

Have you been faced with similar life crisis? Share among your group.

Rizpah's Trusted in God: *"Those who know your name trust in you, for you, Lord, have never forsaken those who seek you" (Psalm 9:10).*

Her trust in God must be prevalent and most evident during this difficult season of her life. The Christian mother, like other believers is tempted to doubt the Lord's hand over her life; yet she remains steadfast in His ability to take care of her and her family's needs. She establishes a trust relationship with God that grows every day.

Rizpah's Faith: *"A faithful person will be richly blessed" (Proverbs 28:20).* Her faith will most certainly be tested in her role as wife and mother. A godly mother will accept the trying of her faith so she can grow in perseverance. She demonstrates her faithfulness as she continues to mature in her relationship with God and others.

Rizpah's Diligence: *We want each of you to show this same diligence to the very end, so that what you hope for may be fully realized. Hebrews 6:11.* A Christian mother finds herself meditating on the Holy Scriptures regularly. She seeks and actively engages the Word of God for every problem in the home. She meditates on the Holy Scriptures regularly as she speaks and teaches them to her children. Her family witnesses her diligence and learns from her example to apply God's teachings to their everyday lives. Rizpah was diligent as she did everything she could to protect even the flesh of her children.

Rizpah's Protection Demonstrates Unconditional Love: *There is no fear in love. But perfect love drives out fear, because fear has to do with punishment. The one who fears is not made perfect in love. 1 John 4:18*

A mother who loves God with all her heart isn't afraid to unconditionally love her children. She understands that her patience may be tried by disobedience, but it will never cause her love to regress in anger. Her love brings confidence in her offspring's since they never worry about loss of love due to bad behaviour.

Ritzpah's Example: *"You are the salt of the earth"* (Luke 5:13). A Christian mother isn't necessarily better than other mothers; but rather she has special seasoning due to the presence of the Holy Spirit. The believing mother has a wealth of resources available to train, discipline, and love her children in the grace of God. She could have justifiably walked away many times, but then she would not be the living example that many of us as women need to persevere, even when we don't know what the end will bring. Does your presence as a mother bring a delightful taste to those around you?

A good Christian mother stays intimately connected with God so that she will keep a discerning heart. She's willing to grow in knowledge through the reading of God's word and absorbing truth from mature godly mothers. God grants her discernment in the lives of her children so that they may be specifically well-trained in righteousness.

A believing mom never gives up on her children. People may want to write off a difficult, rebellious child or one challenged with learning difficulty, but not a praying mother. She will plead the grace and mercy of God over their lives if there's breath in her body. This mother is compelled and encouraged by the Holy Spirit to keeping praying no matter what. I am certain Rizpah prayed continuously throughout this difficult plight.

Rizpah's Sacrifice:

A loving mother many times puts herself last and continues to drive when the rest of the house is still. She realizes that obedience is better than sacrifice. She takes to heart the role God has assigned her to love, care for and nurture her children. And just when you think there is no hope, God reaches down and says "take my hand and let me lead the way. Be still and know that I am God and together we can do anything", even fight off destruction.

The Teaching Plan

The story of Rizpah gives a soul stirring example of what a mother will do when called to care for and protect her children. Some may get focused on the fact that Rizpah was a concubine of Saul's but don't miss the central truth of this lesson; that being that God uses sinners to bring the truth of His love to reality. The passion, drive, vigilance, and faith of this woman is a footprint of God's unyielding love for us. Regardless as to what sins I have committed, God says if you give your life to me, I will use you for my esteemed GLORY!

Opening Student Involvement:

Questions to Ponder (DIG DEEPER):

Can you think of a time in your life when you had to drop or put your goals and aspirations to the side for the welfare and protection of your children?

The Cause: 2 Samuel 21: 1-6

- The Gibeonites Revenged; Famine in the land for 3 years.
- David seeks God. Why does seeking God matter?
- David's Dilemma & The Consequences: 21:4
- What happens when a promise made by the direction of God is broken?
- What was the Gibeonites request?
- What was David's Decision?

The Circumstance: v. 7:7

• What do you do when you are punished for being you?

• What happens when you have no control of your future?

• When innocent people are hurt The Crisis: v. 8-13

• What is the significance of sackcloth? Discuss its symbolism of brokenness.

• Fighting off the enemy.

• The penalty for unattended sin The Celebration: v. 14

• Look at David's compassion.

• Why not a proper Burial for Saul's descendants?

• Rizpah's deliverance.

PRAY FOR MOTHERS

Rizpah- A Mothers' Love

Unscramble words pertinent to this lesson

1. Bisgientoe _____

2. Atnonevc _____

3. Nmoair _____

4. Pesmthhohieb _____

5. etmrsoh veol_____

6. igielcedn_____

7. rstteud odg_____

8. faicecirs_____

9. inemfa_____

10. piahrz_____

Notes Page:

WOMAN OF FAITH – HATTIE TENNISON

Tis So Sweet to Trust in Jesus,
Just to Take Him At His Word,
Just to Rest Upon His Promise;
Just to Know, Thus Saith The Lord.
Jesus, Jesus, How I Trust Him,
How I've Proved Him O'er and O'er,
Jesus, Jesus, Precious Jesus!
O For Grace to Trust Him More.

As I pen these words, the world is experiencing a COVID–19 Pandemic. I am still depending on Jesus' BLOOD to hide me from the virus. In my lifetime I have had to demonstrate Divine Faith many times. This faith that reaches beyond the, "I can do all things through Christ which strengthened me." (Phil. 4:13)

I have seen GOD work, when I didn't know what to do, what to ask for, I couldn't pray, I was just astonished. GOD never failed to bring me through and to work it out. This Divine Faith in GOD, has brought me through many life situations. Being part of a small newly organized church, there have been many times that GOD had to make away, out of what we saw as 'no way'. For example, the establishment of our church after many trials and unfortunate tribulations; having to step out on faith to execute the ministries God had assigned to us, and even members having to finish.

This proves that when you feel a 'no', if you just stand still, don't give up, keep praying, HE will answer, and you will know, that GOD sees and cares for even the least of us. When GOD has brought you through so many obstacles in life, you learn to trust him no matter what, no matter how bad it seems, and no matter how long it takes. HE is Sovereign and HE will Bless you as you rely on the promises in HIS WORD.

Hattie Tennison- member of St. John Missionary Baptist Church, Rev. Dr. Michael Jolla 1st Pastoral Assignment-Greenville, TX

THE SYROPHOENICIAN WOMAN

Read the Scripture: Matthew 15:22-28, Mark 7:24-30

The truths of the Story Introduction:

The Lord smiles (is pleased) when women totally submit their concerns to Him. The old adage "Anyway you bless me Lord, I'll be satisfied" applies!

Why was Jesus in Tyre and Sidon?

This remarkable woman exemplifies courage and a strong faith that can be emulated. Even when it appears that Jesus is not paying attention to us in our times of tragic needs, we should have faith that He will or can respond to our situation. It is a proof point that He wants to know we have total reliance on Him.

The Lord provides a shower of love and smiles when women totally submit their cares and their concerns to Him. This woman did not ask for a 'whole loaf' of blessings, through her dialog, she understood that just the **crumbs from Jesus** were enough to **restore her child** to health.

To understand the full context of this story, we must examine the writer and the writings of the Book of Matthew, including the setting in the beginning of Matthew, chapter 15.

While Matthew is writing primarily to a Jewish audience, providing proof points throughout that Jesus is the Messiah, the fulfiller and fulfilment of God' s promise, this story demonstrates that Jesus does not limit His blessings to any particular race Jew or Gentile, but that it is a ***universal gospel***.

Even to a Phoenician, Baal worshipping woman. The Phoenicians were Greek Semites who became racially mixed and usually worshipped Baal. No love was lost between the Jews and the Phoenicians. See Ezekiel 28 to understand the "prophecy against Tyre".

Earlier in chapter 15, the Pharisees had tried to trap Jesus and Jesus quickly pointed out that Jewish ***rituals*** were not to interfere with ***righteousness***. In other words, don't get so caught into the law that you miss the essence of the law. God is no respecter of person.

Isn't it strange though, that Jesus had just demonstrated his love as a 'universal' love, in verses 1–20, however in verse 23, He did not answer the woman and in verse 24 He answered, I was only sent to the 'lost sheep' of Israel. The scripture in Matthew 15:23 states 'Jesus did not answer a word". Why would Jesus ignore this woman? Why would he have her believe He could not help her? Was He testing her faith? Does He test our faith? What reaction was Jesus looking for? How does the woman respond?

Have you called on Jesus lately? Did he turn His head? What insight can you glean from this woman's actions?

She would not take NO for an answer. She was confident that Jesus COULD heal her daughter, and she was **PERSISTENT** in her **Plea.** "Lord son of David, have mercy on me".

Why didn't she call on **Baal**? How did she know Jewish history and have respect enough to call Jesus, son of David? What are some 'gods' we put our trust and money in? However, when we 'really' need help, we come to the one TRUE Lord God: our **creator** and **sustaining** God.

She needed God's mercy to intervene to restore her daughter to good health. It reminds me of the song of old:

This reminds me of the song ... **"Your grace and mercy brought me through.** I'm living (my daughter) this moment, because of you. I want to THANK YOU, and Praise you too, Your Grace and Mercy, brought me through.

She knew of Jesus' **power**, and she also knew of his **compassion** for those who believe in Him. Romans 10:10 reads, "For with the heart man believeth unto righteousness; and with the mouth confession is made unto salvation," KJV.

Her **persevering, passionate** and **purposeful plea**, provide **an example** to us as Christian women in the 21st century. It is so easy for us to give up, to be defeated and depressed.

This woman knew that Jesus could help her, and she was not willing to accept anything shorter than his healing for her daughter.

Her proposition to Jesus was even more astounding, as she clearly shows she was not asking for MUCH…. she is not being gluttonous; she is not asking for ALL of Jesus' time. She clearly states that she has the faith to know that even a 'crumb falls to dogs', **SURELY** there is a blessing in Jesus for her. What she is basically demonstrating, is that we need to go to him for ALL our needs; He is **the fulfiller** of our NEEDS. In Matthew 17:20b, the scripture states, *"if ye have faith as a grain of mustard seed, ye shall say unto this mountain, remove hence to yonder place; and it shall remove; and nothing shall be impossible unto you"*.

In verse 27, she acknowledges that Jesus was sent for the lost sheep of Israel, however she only wants a little of His blessing. As she puts it, *"but even the dogs eat the crumbs that fall from their master's table"*. What is the 'truth' in the reference to a dog? Is the woman calling herself a 'dog'? The 'truth' here is that when you have purposeful faith, you know that Jesus has enough healing in the 'hem of His garment' to fulfil your needs.

Even after Jesus went away, it did not deter this woman. She followed. She would not let Him go until He blessed her. In the tune of another familiar tune, **"I won't let go 'til you bless me Lord," I'm going to get what you promised me"** or **'Standing on the Promises** of Christ my king; Through eternal ages let His praises ring; Glory in the highest, I will shout and sing; Standing on the promises of God "Jesus felt the sincere passion of this persistent and determined woman's plea. Her profound faith had brought a practical result.

Jesus healed her daughter. 'Without faith, it is impossible to please the Lord! Surely because of her faith, her daughter was healed. She could have given up, but she did not. She kept the faith, even when it appeared her tragic outcome would remain the same. She trusted and believed, and Jesus responded.

Think About it:

What is the significance of Matthew including the story about a **Phoenician** woman?

Look at Jesus as:

- Messiah

- Fulfilment of the Abrahamic Promise

Why is **universal gospel** of significance to us?

Could Jesus had positioned himself to be in Phoenicia just to have an encounter with this woman? Why?

Are we like the Pharisees at times? We get so caught into the **rituals** they interfere with **righteousness**.

Look at the character of this woman:

- The **Person:** A Phoenician woman; why does this matter?

- The **Plea:** Heal my daughter. Can you think of a time the Lord brought you through? What song comes to your mind?

- The **Pause,** Jesus turned away.

- The Passion of Persistent Prayer.

- The **Proposition.**

- The Woman of **Profound** Faith.

- The Practical Result: Jesus will answer prayer…we simply must believe.
- The Praise: Praise God from whom all blessings flow….

Have you praised God lately?

The Teaching Plan

The Syrophoenician Woman

Matthew 15:22-28, Mark 7:24-30

The Lord provides a shower of love and smiles when woman totally submit their cares and the concerns to Him.

Can you think of a time when you believe God smiled about you?

- The **Person**
  - Phoenician Woman.
  - Baal worshipper.
  - She knew Jesus had the POWER.
  - She looked for Jesus' universal LOVE.
- The **Plea** - "I love the Lord; He heard my cry"
  - Purpose—She wanted him to heal her daughter.
  - Why Persevere through life's situation?
  - Passionate—"Son of David" have mercy on me.
  - Pursuing other gods; Why didn't she call on Baal? What other gods interfere with us calling on the 'true' God.
  - She called out to the Provider God (Jehovah Jireh).
- The **Pause**
  - Jesus turned away.
  - What happens when it appears that Jesus has turned away from you?
- The **Passion**
  - Why does Persistent Prayer matter?
  - Jesus has the power – Romans 10:10
- The **Proposition**

- o She was not too proud to ask. Be careful of personal pride. Why?
- The Woman's **Profound Faith.**
  - o She knew it would not take much of Jesus to heal her daughter.
  - o **'Even the dogs" …there is healing in the 'crumbs'**
- **The Practical Result**
  - o Those who hope in the Lord, demonstrate the power of true inner spirituality.
  - o Isaiah 40:31
- The Praise

PRAISE GOD FROM WHOM ALL BLESSINGS FLOW

Write down three things you want to Praise God for:

1. _____

2. _____

3. _____

Now,   **LET'S   PRAISE   HIM!!!!!!!!!!!!!!!!!!!!!!!!!!!!!!!!!!!**

Notes Page:

_____

_____

_____

_____

_____

_____

_____

_____

_____

_____

_____

_____

_____

_____

_____

_____

_____

_____

_____

_____

_____

_____

_____

_____

_____

Summary

It is my prayer that these women of the Bible have been a source of strength and encouragement for you. Their faith, commitment, and dedication are proof points of how to respond when life's issues come your way. Whether challenged with quick thinking to solve a problem, being the sister to help another sister along the way or pushing with persistence to get a blessing from the Lord, each of these women demonstrated Biblical principles we can all emulate.

Why these 7 women examples when there are so many other women in the Bible who are also ripe with examples of Christian fortitude? Each of these women were a source of biblical encouragement for me during various seasons of my life.

Hopefully at least one of them resonated with you in an area you need stronger faith, belief, or perseverance. If not one of these, I encourage you to find some woman in the Bible whose Biblical character and principles can be a motivating factor in your life.

The scripture tells us that God has a purpose and a plan for each of us. It is my prayer that through these women, you found a path to discovering yours.

Thank you for this opportunity to study 7, really 8 extraordinary women of the Bible! I pray victory will be yours!

Sisterly yours.
Sandra

<u>Inspiring Women of the Bible</u>: Crossword

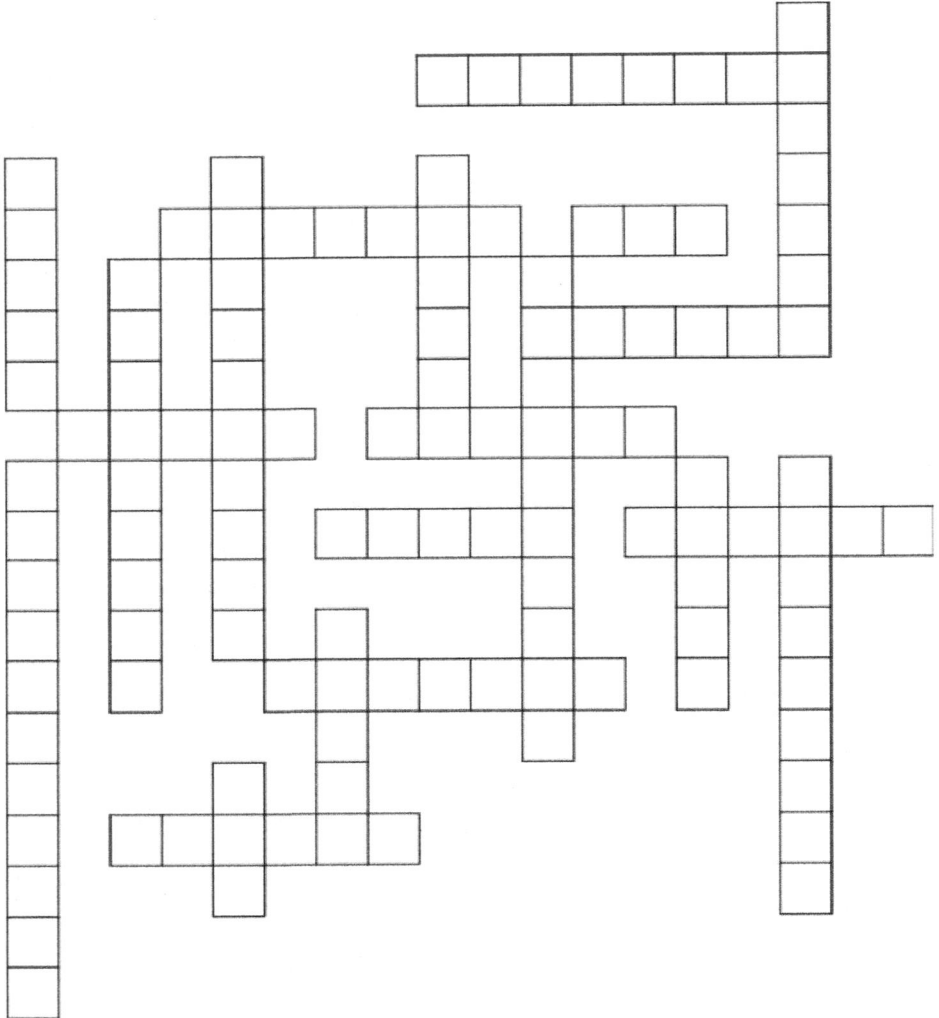

Clues & Answers for Crossword

ACROSS

2. From Moab
3. Pilgrimage by Jews
8. to keep asking
9. show happiness
12. showed mothers love
14. to believe
15. Mediator
19. King of Israel
20. barren woman
23. A woman of beauty
25. laid to rest
26. The king in Ruth
27. to demonstrate belief

DOWN

1. husband of Peninah
4. Seller
5. to continue with zeal
6. Queen who saved her people
7. talking to God
10. Naomi's Disposition
11. Mutual affection
13. to give up something
16. to show smarts
17. stubborn
18. to act on behalf of someone
21. to hurt or manipulate
22. a commitment
24. to weep

Abuse	Nabel	Ruth	Joy
Abigail	Boaz	baptize	Trust
Intercede	Hannah	Priest	intelligent
Prayer	Friendship	Persistent	sacrifice
Festival	buried	Rizpah	Esther
Depressed	promise	Elkanah	Persist
cry	David	Lydia	

BIBLIOGRAPHY AND RESOURCES USED

Bibles:

King James Version
New International Version NIV Serendipity

Books:

"The Seasons of a Woman's Life" – Lois Evans
"All the Women of the Bible" – Herbert Lockyer "The Purpose Driven
Life" – Rick Warren

Reference:

The New International Dictionary of the Bible Webster's Collegiate
Dictionary
Biblegateway.com
          Internet reference
Read more:
https://www.whatchristianswanttoknow.com/12-qualities-of-a-
          christian-mother/#ixzz6If0IbM7z
http://bibleseo.com/christian-life/lydia-seller-purple-
cloth-bible-character-study/

Made in the USA
Coppell, TX
25 January 2021